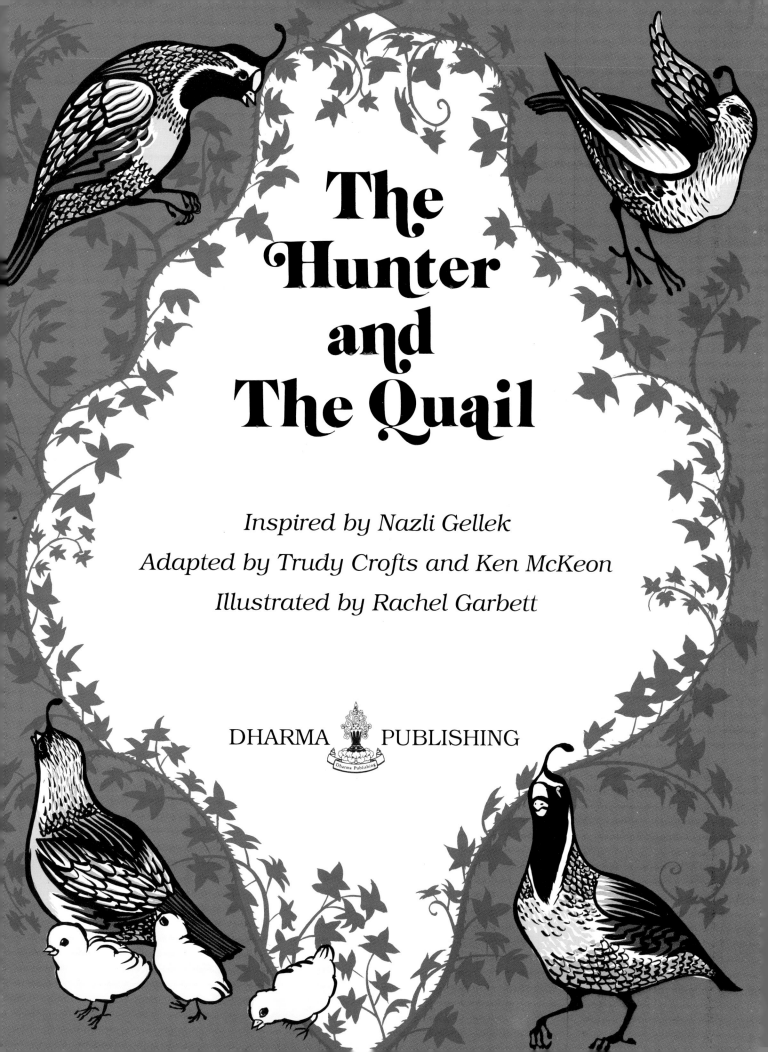

The Hunter and The Quail

Inspired by Nazli Gellek

Adapted by Trudy Crofts and Ken McKeon

Illustrated by Rachel Garbett

DHARMA PUBLISHING

ISBN 0-89800-251-6
ISBN 0-89800-250-8 (pbk)
Revised edition 1993. First published 1976.

Endpapers by Margie Horton

Printed in the United States of America by Dharma Press

Dedicated to

All the World's Children

The Jataka Tales

The Jataka Tales celebrate the power of action motivated by compassion, love, wisdom, and kindness. They teach that all we think and do profoundly affects the quality of our lives. Selfish words and deeds bring suffering to us and to those around us. Selfless actions give rise to goodness of such power that its influence spreads in ever-widening circles, uplifting all forms of life.

The Jataka Tales, first related by the Buddha over two thousand years ago, bring to light his many lifetimes of positive action practiced for the sake of the world. As an embodiment of great compassion, the Awakened One reappears in many forms, in many times and places, to ease the suffering of living beings. Thus the Jataka stories are filled with heroes of all kinds, each demonstrating that compassion and wisdom have the power to transform any situation.

Although based on traditional accounts, the stories in the Jataka Tales Series have been adapted for children of today. May these tales inspire the positive thoughts and actions that will sustain the heart of goodness and illuminate the wisdom of all spiritual traditions for the well-being of future generations.

Tarthang Tulku   Founder, Dharma Publishing

Once there was a very wise quail who could teach all the great family of birds. They called him the Sage. All the birds, including the Sage, lived together in a vast green forest where there were dense thickets in which to hide their nests, clear deep springs for drinking and washing, and seeds of every sort to eat. They were happy living there.

But one day a hunter came into the forest, and he had a net for trapping birds. Far worse than the net, he had a special trick. For he knew how to imitate bird-calls and bird-songs. On this day he sang out a few of those deceiving notes. and the birds, thinking that other birds, friends or relatives perhaps, were calling to them, crept closer and closer to the place of the hunter.

When they were near at hand, the wily hunter slipped the net out from under his coat and flung it over them. The birds were quite surprised and quite trapped. They were piled topsy-turvy in a brown-feathered heap. The satisfied hunter stuffed the birds into his wicker basket and carried them home. He would sell them later in the marketplace.

For many days, the hunter returned to the forest and each time he captured a full net of birds.

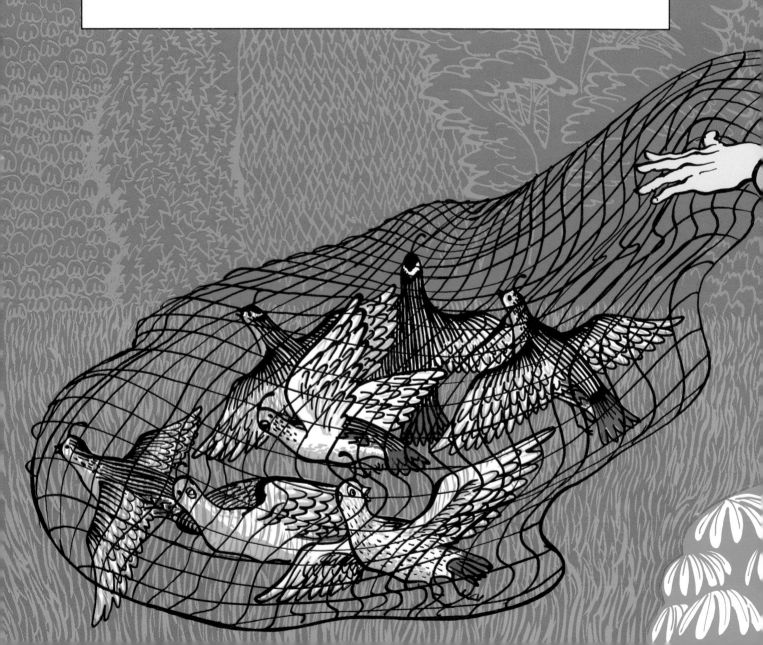

The Sage himself was never trapped, but he was troubled by the cruel hunter. So he called his family together to teach them to escape.

He said, "This tricky hunter thinks that he can trap us all, but we can stop him. Tomorrow when you feel the weight of the net, look at the net; look for a space between the cords. When you find one, thrust your head through. Then beat your wings in a flurry and take to the air. Working together, trusting each other, we can lift the net and fly off with it to the nearest bush. There the net will lie in a tangled heap, and you can wriggle out from underneath."

Since the birds wanted to escape the hunter, they decided to try the Sage's plan. The next morning, the hunter came back to the forest. After placing himself in a thicket, he began to call. Soon a large flock of birds drew near. At once he whisked out his net and cast it over the flock. But before he could bundle the birds into his basket, the net rose into the air and came to rest on a thorn bush, whereupon all the birds scrambled out from underneath. They had escaped! When evening came, the hunter was still untangling his net. He returned home empty-handed.

Day after day, the hunter was outwitted by the birds. Night after night he came home with an empty basket. Now the hunter had a wife, and she was angry with him for his failures.

She finally said to him, "Every night you return without any birds. You must be a foolish hunter. We shall surely starve."

"Oh no, my dear," replied her husband, "I am not a fool. These birds have tricked me by working together. But it is hard to cooperate forever. Soon they will lose trust and begin to squabble. And then I will trap them. Birds shall be back in my basket and a smile back on your face."

Sure enough, it was not long afterwards that one of the quail flew down to the forest floor and landed on another bird's head.

"Who stepped on my head?" cried the dazed quail, shaking his crest.

"I did," said the other, "but it was an accident. And besides, you stood right beneath me."

"Don't blame it on me, you stupid bird. You would fly into fire and think it was water."

"Don't call me stupid. I suppose that you think you're so smart you could escape the hunter yourself."

The Sage overheard this bickering back and forth. He thought to himself,

"If the birds turn to such quarreling they will no longer be able to lift the net. Yet still my family must be safe. So those who wish to live in peace I shall take with me and we can learn to trust one another. Together we can overcome the threat of any hunter, no matter how clever he is." Then the Sage and his flock departed.

The next day the hunter returned. He gave out his call. The birds that had chosen to remain behind listened and drew near him. Then the hunter flung his net over them. Now was the moment for working together, for flying off to safety. Instead, the birds argued.

One said to the other, "You never help with the net. That's not fair. You should do more."

The other answered, "I do more than you, you jabbering bunch of feathers. This time it's your turn to work harder."

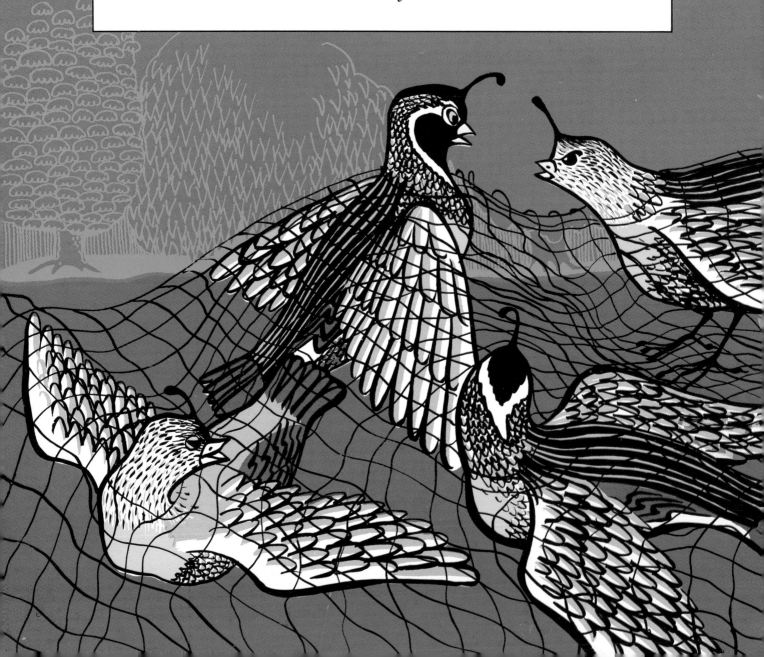

And while the two birds insulted and ordered each other about, the hunter gathered them up and stuffed those foolish creatures into his basket. He took them home to a happy wife.

So it was in ancient times that quarreling birds were captured by the hunters, but those who learned to work together could escape the cleverest foe.

My page

Colored by _____

The Jataka Tales Series